The Thinking Person's Limerick Book

With Author Comments
Not Your Usual Stuff
None X Rated

---

by Gene Brandt

Published by GB Books

Printed and bound by 48 Hour Books

Copyright © 2013 by Gene Brandt

All rights reserved. No part of this book may be reproduced or transmitted in any form or by any means without written permission from the author.

Cover design by Alexandra Brandt

ISBN: 978-0-615-92222-5

Published by GB Books

Printed in USA by 48HrBooks (www.48HrBooks.com)

Dedication

This book is dedicated to the Monday Morning Boys, a small group of retired professors from Southwestern Illinois College who meet each Monday for breakfast. The purpose of our meetings is to solve the world's problems and try to outdo each other with funny stuff. I was affiliated with this college for 32 years.

Table of Contents

Dedication ---------------------------------- iii
Table of Contents ---------------------------- iv
Foreword ------------------------------------- 1
Chapter 1 Bad Guys ------------------------ 3
Chapter 2 Dumb Guys --------------------- 9
Chapter 3 Unfortunate People ------------ 27
Chapter 4 Education ---------------------- 31
Chapter 5 Sports ---------------------------- 39
Chapter 6 Travel ---------------------------- 43
Chapter 7 Monday Morning Boys -------- 49
Chapter 8 People I Know (Or Know Of)-- 55
Chapter 9 Almost Everybody Else -------- 61
Chapter 10 PG Rated ------------------------ 83

Foreword

A limerick is a simple poetic form consisting of five lines in which lines 1, 2, and 5 rhyme and lines 3 and 4 rhyme with a different sound. I have taken no lessons in this poetic form nor have I studied it in a class or book, but believe I have mastered the basics. Writing good limericks requires a sense of rhythm and rhyme. I have read hundreds of limericks that are terrible because the rhythm is not there or the rhyming is bad or both. Also the writer should realize that what he or she is writing is a mini story and each of the five lines should pertain to the story. The best limericks have a line five that is a surprise or call it a zinger and though this is difficult, I think that many of the ones in this book achieve it.

Many limericks are obscene and you won't find any of them in this book. Some of them, however, are a bit risqué and I have put them in a section labeled PG Rated so that a very sensitive person can avoid them.

Each limerick is preceded by an author comment, some intended to be funny and some informative.

Gene

Chapter 1 - Bad Guys

Many limericks are about bad guys. Here is a sampling.

Did you ever get cheated by a big company? I have.

Big business says look here's the deal
Our mantra is lie, cheat, and steal,
   To hell with the folks
   Those ignorant blokes
If you tax us were sure to appeal.

I think Jose's wife liked money more than she liked Jose.

Jose Ramon Bolivar
Was struck and killed by a car.
   His wife didn't cry
   As hard as she'd try
Her inheritance was way above par.

Many people think of the British Royal Family as welfare recipients? If you think about it, they get tax money to do - - - what?

The Royal family gets high pay
They don't work, mostly play,
   They suck up tax dough
   Then act as though
They do something useful each day.

<u>*Joe was not a very nice guy but he certainly made Yvonne happy.*</u>

Track tout Joe worked his con
On those he could work it on,
   The suckers they came
   Dumb and smart just the same
And he spent all their dough on Yvonne.

That Dracula fella is one mean dude. The guy in question here will need a bandage on his backside.

Count Dracula dressed all in black
Sometimes stretched folks on the rack
   Then sank his big teeth
   Into their underneath
And for good measure gave them a whack.

Jail is the ultimate fate of ladies like this one.

She's a whiz at keeping the books,
There's nothing she overlooks.
   She can cook them too,
   She's now in a stew
And has become one of the crooks.

It's time for a history lesson. Louis XVI of France became king at age 19. He was an immature and indecisive leader. He was executed for treason in 1793.

Louis sixteenth it is said,
To Marie Antoinette was wed,
  But the trouble he had
  With his people was bad
And Louis sixteenth lost his head.

Lesson two, Henry VIII of England. Henry number eight was crowned king at age 17. As the years went by he became a fat old guy with a fixation on changing wives after killing the previous one.

Henry the eighth was quite mad,
His wives would discover how bad,
  He killed them all
  The short and the tall
And they lost everything that they had.

This guy Jose apparently had a Mexican mother and a Scottish father. He also seemed to be an excellent cusser in multiple languages.

Jose Gonzalez McLish
Got his TV from a dish.
  In storms it went out
  And Jose would shout
Obscenities in Spanish.

And Jose had odd epicurean tastes. This food is for some people but not me.

Jose was an ugly galoot
Who ate truckloads of pig snoot.
  I would donate
  The snoots that he ate
To people who live in Beirut.

Chapter 2 - Dumb Guys

Limericks about dumb people abound, here is my collection of them.

People who talk too much are a real pain.

A woman named Bernadette Bavver
Was guilty of constant palaver.
  She talked a blue streak
  Always flapping her beak
And that's why no man'll have 'r.

<u>Lester is obviously a dunce, also a dead one.</u>

A man named Lester McLound
Put on two parachutes he found.
  He jumped out the door
  With confidence galore
Had they opened he'd still be around.

Too bad because Angus is not rich.

Angus McPhillie McGee
Drove his car into a tree.
  His auto it did
  Go into a skid
And repairs ain't gonna be free.

Sometimes practical jokes are not advisable.

A Frenchman named Pierre Le Blanc
Decided to pull off a prank,
  Gave an exploding cigar
  To a friend in his car
And got hit in the head with a plank.

You can't always tell how tough a guy is by looking.

A tough looking guy named Stan
Thought he was superman
   But he wore out quickly
   Then looked kind of sickly
He was just a flash in the pan.

Festus Haggin was one of my favorite characters from the old and long running Gunsmoke *TV show. He didn't have much learnin' but was wise in the ways of the world.*

Festus Haggin was taught by his Maw
And good grammar sticks in his craw,
   As to headlights by day
   Festus would say
It ain't seein' its gitten saw.

Politeness counts but sometimes it's impossible.

A fellow named Harley McCoo
Loved spaghetti along with ragu.
   Around his spoon he would twirl
   But it would always unfurl
So he slurped it like me and you.

You can change over time if you don't take care of yourself.

LuLu LaFemme looked quite nice,
That prompted the men to look twice
   But over the years
   After too many beers
They say that one look will suffice.

Some states have laws against phony heroes, Hugh was guilty of Stolen Valor.

Wounded in battle was Hugh
So we must give him his due,
   He cut open his head
   When he tripped on a bed
And for a purple heart he will sue.

You don't have to have a good figure to wear a bikini.

Rarely does anyone care
What girls at the beach will wear
   But at 300 pounds
   Loretta has found
Her swimsuit just makes people stare.

<u>*Wasting time in college does have consequences*</u>

Joe Floogle's college career
Was mostly just drinking beer.
   His time there was brief
   His grades brought him grief
And employers turned a deaf ear.

<u>*Changing your mind at the altar doesn't usually involve marrying a saint.*</u>

"Help me St. Patrick", she said
As she was about to be wed.
   "My husband to be
   Is not right for me."
So she married the saint instead.

Rupert was our guide in Ireland and his wife was overweight. We wrote some limericks as our bus approached the town of Limerick and asked Rupert if we could use the microphone to entertain our fellow travelers, he said no. Maybe he thought they would be dirty.

Young Rupert the Ireland guide
Has a wife about six feet wide,
   He hugs her in parts
   Then gets back where he starts
And sometimes with others collide.

I actually knew some folks in the old home town who thought the world was flat.

It dawned on old Cletus McGee
That with science he didn't agree,
   The earth is flat
   And that is that
So just look and its plain to see.

Where you do it sometimes makes all the difference.

Harley, a fun loving man
In the street played kick the can.
  The can it was loaded
  And it exploded
He was playing in Afghanistan.

A guy like Stan has to expect a bad outcome.

The famous old daredevil Stan
Went over the falls in a can,
  The can hit a rock
  And knocked off his block
The funeral was held in Spokane.

Well, her intentions were good.

Rosie went out to give blood,
She fell on her face with a thud.
   The blood that she gave
   No sick man would crave
It was all on the ground in the mud.

The wheels of justice work slowly except once in a while.

Henrietta from St. Louis MO
Was in need of some serious dough.
   She pulled a bank job
   And a teller named Bob
Pulled a gun and struck a death blow.

<u>Are you sure that's what Jesus would do?</u>

The Reverend Arthur La Flag
Said, "I am loath to brag
  But hell and damnation
  Are my fixation
And condemning folks is my bag."

<u>Take a good look at the 2nd amendment boys, read the part about militias.</u>

Don't take my guns away
Said Hank from the NRA,
  I've got 15 long guns
  To shoot off your buns
And people are fair game I say.

There are rules about drinking and flying but if you're going to break the rules, this pilot landed in the right place.

An airplane crashed in the bush
The pilot? He injured his tush
   He drank beer that day
   And some people say
He landed at Anheuser Busch.

Some people are just too dumb to explain things to.

Herkimer Herman Malone
Wanted to pilot a drone.
   Look you hayseed
   For a drone there's no need,
With no pilot is how it is flown.

<u>Joe is one of those unfortunate people who just can't seem to get the hang of relating to girls.</u>

The bartender at Joe's Moonlight Bar
Admired the girls from afar,
  He'd tell them a joke
  And light up their smoke
But the girls thought him not up to par.

<u>Don't hire this guy to be your cook.</u>

The cook made some corned beef hash
And served the stuff up in a flash.
  By eating it you could
  And probably would
Go to the john in a mad dash.

Divorce the guy!

Olaf worked at the mall,
He cleaned out the toilet stall.
  His wife thought him crude
  When this ignorant dude
Refused to bathe at all.

Mortimer Snerd was one of Edgar Bergen's
ventriloquist dummies in show biz long ago.
He was a country bumpkin.

Mortimer Snerd is his name,
Stupidity's his claim to fame.
  He's dumb as can be
  And oh lordy me
Whatever he tries turns out lame.

Some folks are perpetual skeptics with twisted logic. Nothing the government does could possibly be true.

"Hope springs eternal", said Sue
Sue said some silly things too,
   Like, "The earth is flat
   And I really think that,
Moon landings are quite untrue."

I wonder if Jeremy has tried AA.

Jeremy Wilkerson's night
Was drinking till he got tight,
   He'd stumble around
   And lie on the ground
And sometimes get into a fight.

<u>I once had a guide in Spain who ate so much garlic it came out of his pores, You could smell him from several feet away.</u>

"Holy Toledo" said Jan
"Why can't I find me a man,
   I'm pretty enough
   And give them no guff",
But Jan was a big garlic fan.

<u>Don't put your money in this bank!</u>

A dumb man who worked in a bank
Went out to sea in a tank.
   The tank didn't float,
   It wasn't a boat,
It was caused by how much he drank.

Olaf was probably texting and driving, maybe also e-mailing his girlfriend.

Olaf Swanson the Swede
Drove down the road at great speed.
   The car hit a tree
   Unlucky is he,
That the speed sign he failed to read.

Not everyone who claims to be a handyman is one.

A handyman once said to me
I can fix your things wait and see.
   He worked on my clock
   And also my lock,
They are now broken permanently.

Why can't people learn to check their equipment before they leave?

Out in the open sea,
The captain said woe is me.
  A hole in the boat
  Made it not float,
To the lifeboat they did flee.

Who was in charge of this lifeboat, Mortimer Snerd?

The lifeboat was missing an oar,
They had one but needed one more.
  They pulled up a plank
  And the lifeboat sank
They had pulled it up from the floor.

That's a good excuse, Bo, do you think they'll buy it?

Bo Fink was arrested one day,
A traffic fine he didn't pay.
  "It wasn't my fault,
   My old cousin Walt
Was driving" we heard Bo say.

Listen, Henry, why don't you try overeaters anonymous?

Henry said "How on earth
Did I acquire this girth?"
  "No mystery to me",
   Said his wife Marie.
"You eat everything on earth."

Frankly, Joe, I think you could get some help from AA.

At Joe's bar one night was seen
A drunk who was getting quite mean.
  He thought that this space
   Was a transport place
And said, "When's the next bus to Racine?"

Chapter 3 – Unfortunate People

This is my collection of limericks about unfortunate people.

Being pulled apart is no fun as Boris found out.

Boris was stretched on the rack,
He was quite taken aback
  And what is worse
  He would need a hearse
If they didn't cut him some slack.

Flies carry bad germs you know.

Tyrone got quite a surprise,
What fell into his soup was flies.
  He tried Pepto Biz
  And a seltzer fiz
But they couldn't prevent his demise.

I found out that my doctor's hobby is motorcycle riding and I had thought it might be stamp collecting. Here is one for him.

A motorcycle's a dangerous thing
When a rider's out on a fling,
  The chance he will die
  Goes up very high
And bells up in heaven may ring.

My friend Jim's home town is Gratz, Kentucky. I borrowed his home town for this one.

An insurance salesman from Gratz
Said "Your house is ridden with rats.
  A policy you need
  For all pests indeed
Including those miserable bats."

Don't mope! Do something constructive.

Wallow in misery if you wish,
What a fine kettle of fish.
   You won't have a friend
   And then in the end
Nothing your life will accomplish.

I was the youngest of 10, Lulu, so I know what its like to be left out.

Little sister Lulu has said,
"Why is it when I go to bed,
   Big sis, she stays up
   To laugh and cutup
And cavort with her boyfriend Fred."

This made John Henry feel much better about himself. Wouldn't it make us all feel better.

This fellow John Henry Le Blanc
Had a life that was in the tank.
   Quite a sad sack
   Was this stupid hack
Till he inherited a bank.

A lady can't be too careful about who she dates.

The curly haired lady looked great
While out on the town with a date,
   Her date got too rough
   And acted so tough
That her curly hair was scared straight.

Chapter 4 – Education

Since I was in education for 51 years I had to create this category.

This is especially true if the old man has to use an outdoor toilet in the winter time.

Some folks call a pee cahn a pee can,
Is it a nut or some kind of pan.
   I'm sure I know
   What a pee can is though,
It's a bedside jar for an old man.

Most inventions are done by people who have creative minds.

A man who's resourceful and wise
Would quickly, I think we'd surmise,
   Invent something nice
   Without thinking twice
And better than most would devise.

<u>In far too many cases the perpetrator gets less punishment than the victim.</u>

Our justice system they say
Makes all the criminals pay.
   When they're in a stew
   They'll get there due,
But does it work? I say no way.

<u>Why is it that today's song writers use only a few words and repeat them over and over and over?</u>

Modern lyrics are easy to write
So why are we old folks uptight?
   It's plain to see
   Why that would be,
The vocabulary needed is slight.

How many of these people are found in Tangier?

There was a young man from Tangier
Whose talents it would appear,
  When put to the test
   Were among the best
So he chose a science career.

I certainly hope it does!

Holistic medicine's the rage,
In which many people engage.
  Healing the bod
  With herbs may seem odd
But some think it puts off old age.

<u>Teachers are called upon to do things other than educate.</u>

A teacher from Arlington Heights
Would stop boys from having their fights.
  The boys would say "Sir,
  We do not concur
For fighting is one of our rights."

<u>It may date back to the Ming Dynasty but it doesn't always work.</u>

A Chinese Doctor named Ling
Said "Acupuncture's the thing,
  It'll fix your back
  If it's out of whack,
It dates back to dynasty Ming."

If necessary look them up in the dictionary.

Plethora, modicum, and Dearth;
Least understood words on earth.
  Plethora's a lot,
  Dearth is not
And modicum takes a middle berth.

This limerick tells it like it is. Some people have stood right beside it and asked, "where is it?"

Welcome to old San Antone,
For the Alamo it is well known,
  Surrounded by city,
  The site's not as pretty
As it was when it stood all alone.

It would take a while just to learn how to spell it.

I think that I shall never be
Good at oceanography,
   The branches are many
   And I don't think that any
Would be of much interest to me.

Have you known a teacher like this one? I have.

The professor they say is unfair,
His grading will lead to despair
   His little pop quiz
   Would baffle a whiz,
To pass his class is quite rare.

Sometimes you can't think of a blasted thing to write!

An author will sometimes decry,
"My creative juices are dry,
  I've hit a brick wall,
  My brain's in a stall,
No meaningful phrase can I buy."

Not only do authors run dry but professors do too.

Professor Bob racked his brain,
The lecture he couldn't sustain.
  His mind it went blank,
  For that he can thank
His habit of drinking champagne.

Do you remember your history? We learned in history class that Prince Henry the Navigator ran a school of navigation in Portugal in which he taught the great explorers in the 15th and 16th centuries how to navigate the great oceans. Current thinking among scholars is that there is no evidence that this is true.

Henry the Navigator tried
To point the way east bonafide,
  But some would insist
  He didn't exist,
They seem to think somebody lied.

See, it's easy.

Limericks are easy to make
If you are a bit of a flake,
  The rhyme must be there
  And rhythm to spare
And some poetic license to take.

Chapter 5 – Sports

<u>I was a baseball player and came within three of being in the major leagues, I couldn't 1. field, or 2. hit, or 3. throw.</u>

Archie "the Tiger" McFall
Was quite good at playing baseball,
   He hit and he threw
   And fielded well too
But not good enough for the Hall.

<u>Albert had been known as the best player in baseball during his 11 years with St. Louis. When his contract was up he chose to go to the Los Angeles Angels for 10 years at 24 million a year and he was a declining player by that time.</u>

Al Pujols, St. Louis' straight arrow,
Left town for mucho dinero.
   Taint the money sez he.
   That's a lie sez me.
To haul the dough takes a wheel barrow.

Rick's first year as a rookie pitcher for the Cardinals was great. His fast ball was stunning. Suddenly he couldn't throw strikes but was good at wild pitches. He later re-invented himself as an outfielder.

Rick Ankiel's fast ball was great
He just couldn't find the plate.
  His throws were erratic,
  From fans he got static
But his outfield throws were straight.

I'm with you, Sadie.

From the standpoint of Sadie McFall,
There's no game to watch like baseball,
  Time limit, there's none
  The thrilling home run
And don't forget the boys in the Hall.

George, what would help both of us is either 1. raise the basket three feet or 2. not allow anyone over 5' 6" to play basketball.

Basketball guy George Love
Could not when push came to shove,
   Do the one thing
   That fame would bring
Drop the ball in from above.

He was one of those rare celebrities who lived up to his hype and then some.

Stan Musial was loved by St. Loo,
His records were matched by few,
   Always upbeat
   And willing to greet
Any fan, even me and you.

Chapter 6 - Travel

We love to travel and after I retired in 1993 we did so extensively.

In Portugal in 2002 we stayed a week in Cascais, just north of Lisbon, then went to the southern Algarve coast for a week in Albufeiras.

Cascais was a nice place for me,
A good place for our group to be.
   We cut our stay short
   And by public transport
Went to Albufeira on the sea.

We enjoyed a five day Yangtze River boat ride in China in 2000.

A Yangtze River boat ride
With your sweetie alongside
   Is much fun afloat
   As long as your boat
Does not with others collide.

Buying insurance for an expensive trip may save you mucho dinero.

To buy insurance for a trip
Did out of my mind just slip.
  I forgot just this once
  And felt like a dunce,
Got sick and missed boarding the ship.

In 1997 we did an around the world trip that included a fly by of Mount Everest out of Katmandu, Nepal.

At 29,000 feet and more
Mt. Everest you can't ignore,
  It's a site I saw
  That struck me with awe
And stays with me forevermore.

Jose was the cautious type.

Our guide in Spain was Jose,
He would be with us each day,
   If we agree
   To pay his fee
And if in advance we would pay.

Riding a horse in the congested area around Trafalgar Square is not advisable.

A man at Trafalgar Square
Riding a spirited mare
   Was thrown to the ground,
   His head it was crowned
And he injured his fat derriere.

For those of you who are not seafaring old salts, Davy Jones Locker is the deep blue sea.

Jack sailed his ship 'round the horn,
In stormy seas it was torn.
   The ship it went down
   And they all would drown,
Into Davy Jones Locker borne.

How many times must I tell you, Check your boat before you leave!

An elderly man from Chenote
Went out to sea in a boat,
   Bad luck it would peak
   When the boat sprang a leak,
His chance to survive is remote.

When we were in Hawaii it struck me that since the islands are so small what would you do after you see the whole thing once or twice or three times? It would be costly to fly somewhere else to see something different.

To Oahu went Ralph and his wife
To live there and have a good life.
   The whole thing went sour
   Because in one hour
You can see the whole island twice.

If you see the island and more,
What will be your encore?
   To go elsewhere
   It must be by air,
Soon Oahu's a terrible bore.

Chapter 7 The Monday Morning Boys

These "boys" are in their 60's, 70's, and 80's and retired from Southwestern Illinois College, a motley crew who enjoy each other's company for breakfast every Monday morning. They love to solve the world's problems and outdo each other with funny stuff. Eckert's is a country restaurant in Belleville, Illinois. Here are two limericks about these meetings.

A bunch of old men will meet
Each Monday at 9 to eat.
   Their talk is incessant
   Its quality pubescent
And none of it worth a repeat.

These men get together to dine
At Eckert's each monday at 9.
   Their talk will evolve
   Around problems to solve,
Their opinions may differ from thine.

Jim's home town is tiny Gratz, Kentucky. During the depression of the 1930's his father started a phone company there. It went broke because no one could pay their bill. I tease Jim about his phone company which I call Gratz AT&T.

A major shareholder is he
In the firm Gratz AT&T.
  He's tall and slim,
  His name is Jim
And a mighty fine fellow he be.

Lynn and his wife, Lucy, are the traveling champions of this group. They have been everywhere.

Mr. Lynn, he travels a lot
To most every exotic spot
  But Lucy has said
  No tents just a bed
And only an indoor pot.

Ray is one of the youngest of our group. He plays in volleyball leagues.

He comes from old Abilene,
He's into the volleyball scene.
   Because he's quite tall,
   Ray spikes the ball
So hard it looks like a bean.

I went to Oceanside, California to visit my twin brother and found it colder than usual. While there I got sick and used the services of an urgent care center.

They say Southern CA is nice,
Not a chance for snow or ice,
   Even so I froze
   My little twinky toes
And went to urgent care twice.

A guy should watch his weight when eating out.

Breakfast on Monday's a cinch
To add to your waist 'bout an inch,
   Biscuits and gravy galore,
   Big fat muffins and more,
To get out of the chair takes a winch

This is a pipe dream!

The Monday Morning Boys say
Lets do something for pay,
   A business let's start
   Run like Wal Mart,
It'll lead to a big pay day.

When in the army at Fort Sill, Oklahoma in 1953 I was temporarily assigned to take sound equipment to the rifle range and stay all day. This was a strange assignment for a guy who knew nothing about sound equipment and had trouble finding the rifle range. The rifle fire deafened me for several days.

To the rifle range Gene went each day,
I mean every day come what may.
   His hearing went bad
   And that poor lad
Could not hear what people would say.

For several years I road my bicycle for long distances. In the year 2000 I rode 4,000 miles. I have abandoned that hobby.

Old Gene soon turns 84,
His bicycle sits by the door.
   With wife by his side
   He'll no longer ride
But other things he will explore.

<u>This was the task I laid out for myself when I started writing limericks for this book.</u>

With two hundred limericks to go,
Gene's creative juices would flow.
   Writing them fast
   From first one to last
Mistakes are blamed on a typo.

Chapter 8 – People I Know (Or Know Of)

<u>Clyde was my boss when I set up and ran a teacher aide training program.</u>

A Belleville schoolman named Clyde
Could not sinners abide
  But he divorced his wife
  To start a new life
And no longer sinners deride.

<u>Gordon was a dean at the college who quit to work on new battery technology. I own a lot of stock in the company.</u>

Gordon's a millionaire to be,
It takes time but just wait and see.
  I hope he gets it
  Before his exit
Then Gene is also home free.

Chris worked at Southwestern Illinois College for many years. She married a man who became an alderman in Belleville, Illinois and ran unsuccessfully for mayor.

Christine's ambition was plain,
First lady of Belleville to gain.
   To covet that job
   Said one old town snob
She surely must be insane.

My brother, Jack, is an excellent photographer. He studied under a protégé of Ansel Adams.

Photographer Jack was quite good,
Took pictures in his neighborhood,
   But oh lordy me
   Too bad that he
Didn't make it his livelihood.

The only solution is get a new printer. They are not expensive, the ink is.

I have been printing a lot
And my printer just went to pot,
   It gurgled and heaved
   And got me quite peeved
Because now printing, I'm not.

Whitey Herzog, baseball Hall of Famer, does a TV commercial for a hearing aid company. His wife, Mary Lou, is beside him and just looks at him.

Whitey H. could talk a blue streak,
So smart he could talk for a week.
   Mary Lou said Hey you,
   Let me talk too
Or your life at home will be bleak.

Do you remember the old Popeye the Sailor Man cartoons?

Popeye the sailor man
Ate spinach out of a can.
   He doesn't boast
   But you may be toast
'Cause he can lick any man.

My father swore this was true. When you have no money you eat what is available.

Lard sandwiches my papa said,
They ate with mom's home made bread,
   With salt on top
   Twas not quite slop,
They hoped for better days ahead.

Jack was a widower.

Brother Jack, 84 or so
Sought women born long ago.
   Old girls that he sought
   Were ones that he thought
Had bad hearts and bundles of dough.

Here is another one about my friend Gordon who does all he can to produce a revolutionary new battery.

Gordon the battery man
Does everything that he can
   To produce no less
   Than complete success,
Well anyway that is his plan.

Like most other aspiring millionaire country singers, this guy probably went to Nashville in a hundred dollar car.

A man from old San Jose
Bought a fine guitar to play.
   He tuned it up nice
   Then took lessons twice
And went off to Nashville they say.

Of course he wanted to cover his bones, If you ride a horse bare naked it would surely hurt.

A cowboy named Josephus Jones
Took out a series of loans.
   He needed a horse
   And a pistol of course
And something to cover his bones.

Leave it to a goof off to figure out a way to get away with it.

The graveyard shift was for Jack,
On that one you get less flack.
   The boss does not loom,
   He's in bed we assume,
A goof off will not get the sack.

If you've seen one lazy jackass you've seen 'em all

A donkey who's name is Huff
Wouldn't get off of his duff,
   He refuses to move
   Which just goes to prove
You can't train old Huff enough.

<u>Whether he's a thief or not depends on whether he's with your party or theirs.</u>

All hail the commander in chief,
Opponents may think he's a thief
  But he may persevere
  At least in the year
Of an election that won't bring him grief.

<u>A romantic relationship is bound to have its ups and downs.</u>

Romance is a curious thing,
Who knows what thoughts it will bring.
  You may feel ecstatic
  Or miserable emphatic
But I think your moods will swing.

Always check the label and your wallet.

Organic foods are the rage,
To buy it you need a good wage.
   To grow it for sure
   You need some manure
And a farmer who's on the same page.

A guy never knows what he'll get with a redhead but isn't that also true with brunettes and blonds?

A man named Oliver Rice
Would never have to think twice
   Before he would stare
   At girls with red hair
But to date them's a roll of the dice.

<u>There must be a guy somewhere who could love Juanita.</u>

Juanita was ugly as sin,
She longed for the crowd that was in
   But her face it was sad,
   Her backside was bad
And her front side had many a chin.

<u>Way back in the thirties there was a popular radio show called Fibber McGee and Molly, though I don't think Fibber ever took up with Marie.</u>

Molly said "look here McGee
I feel that you don't quite see
   The trouble your in
   Right up to your chin
Cavortin' with that lady Marie."

Walk softly around these ladies, boys, or you may not be long for this world.

Hell hath no fury like woman scorned,
Men who do this may soon be mourned.
  In this regard
  They'll come down hard
So all men be forewarned.

Men like Fernando should probably avoid marriage.

Fernando, a lady's man he,
As nattily dressed as can be.
  The girls they would flock
  To this sexy Jock
Till Fernando's wife they would see.

If a dog is man's best friend, is a cat a woman's best friend?

Old Shep made everyone see
What loyalty really could be.
   Now a dog's life is sad
   But Old Shep's was not bad
As everyone's friend was he.

I found out later that my brain did not freeze after 200 limericks.

How do I keep writing these
Limericks that may no one please?
   My fear is that my
   Brain will run dry
And go into a permanent freeze.

<u>*Sometimes you just have to live with that aching back.*</u>

Fred went to the doctor to see
What this ache in his back could be.
   The doc said, "My son"
   You may be the one
Who can never afford my fee."

<u>*Soloman's nickname in school was "Skinny".*</u>

Soloman Henry McRidge
Liked to say "I eat just a smidge."
   A smidge is not a lot
   So Soloman is not
Going to have much food in the fridge.

<u>The ignition on Gene's brain was faulty.</u>

I can't think what to write
To make limericks tonight.
   I'm down on my knees
   With an awful brain freeze
My brain I must re-ignite.

<u>Listen, Ralph, you must remember to only patronize bona-fide, certified seed growers.</u>

Ralph the gardner just might
Plant some petunias tonight,
   But the seeds that he had
   Turned out to be bad,
The chance that they'll grow is slight.

The rent comes first then romance if possible.

A feisty old man said he'd find
Some woman who wouldn't mind
   Paying half the rent
   And t'would be heaven sent
If she was romantically inclined.

Mack wasn't actually a teenager, he just acted like one.

Teenage Mack at 84
Thought he'd found a girl to adore,
   She said I don't know
   If You'll be my beaux
And then she walked out the door.

When hermits go into the real world they are sometimes shocked at how times have changed.

Herman the hermit had hives,
A problem that messed up folks lives.
   He went to the doc
   And got quite a shock
When his four figure bill arrives.

Most folks don't know what a flugelhorn is but Fanny did as did the folks who had to listen to it.

The musician, Fannie McDougal,
Played a horn that's called a flugel.
   She played sour notes
   That sounded like goats,
Folks said please switch to a bugle.

All chefs should have a good smeller.

Said Chef Pierre Andre Chappell,
"I can tell good food by the smell.
  If it doesn't smell right
  I will gird for a fight."
But poor Pierre couldn't smell well.

If you haven't come across poet Waddy Mitchell, check him out. Waddy was a real cowboy in his time. My favorite Waddy poem is called "Typical", look it up.

Some poets write of the old West,
Waddy Mitchell I think is the best,
  His poems they rhyme,
  Well most of the time,
Most critics I think will attest.

<u>You learn a lot from reading limericks, like what we import from Uzbekistan.</u>

A fop's what they called Dapper Dan,
His dress was the best in Spokane.
   He wore fancy hats
   And other things that's
Imported from Uzbekistan.

<u>Do four syllable words make you cuss?</u>

Big words like tumultuous
Are enough to make people cuss,
   The syllables are many,
   A lot more than any
Small words folks use to discuss.

"You dames are all alike" said Bogart

In old movies they called girls dames
And Bogart would call them worse names.
   Girls didn't object,
   It was back then correct
But today's girls won't play those games.

It was the German Pope, Benedict XVI.

Alphonse Aloysius McGee
Went to the Vatican to see
   The Pope who was out
   Eating sausage and kraut
On a ship that was far out to sea.

I was thinking of Congressman Anthony Wiener who showed us his private parts on the internet.

I think I will never see
A headline that pleases me.
   They're all about crime
   Most all of the time
Or pols acting creepily.

Actually as much as $3,000 per ear. I'm glad Joe only had two ears.

Joe's favorite word was WHAT?
Good hearing he had not.
   He decided to go
   To a hearing aid pro
But to buy them would cost a lot.

It just makes a girl feel good!

A girl from the suburbs would go
Into the city to blow
  Money on shoes
  And things that amuse
Like clothing that doesn't show.

This is based on an old joke that boys would pull on stores that sell tobacco. Prince Albert was a brand of pipe tobacco that came in a handsome can.

"Do you have Prince Albert in a can?"
Queried Joe at a store in Cheyenne.
  "Yes," said the guy,
  "Do you wish to buy?"
"No, let him out, FREE THE MAN!"

<u>Olaf's ancestors were from various parts of the world and there were differences of opinion.</u>

Olaf Jose Muamar McGee
Had a varied family tree.
   When they would meet
   To break bread and greet
None of them could ever agree.

<u>It would be good if we didn't fight wars in those places.</u>

Uncle Sam says he wants you,
But not just any will do,
   You have to be smart
   Enough to take part
In a war where they speak Urdu.

Of course my lady would never do a thing like that.

I think I'll never understand
Why women will always demand
   That we buy a fur
   And more stuff for her
When I can't afford a hat band.

I do hope you remember Dorothy, the Tin Man, the Cowardly Lion, and the Scarecrow.

Dorothy left Kansas in a blow,
Well actually a tornado
   But her red shoes
   She later would use
To get back to her Kansas chateau.

You never know how you will react until you get there.

Joining up just seemed right,
Marlow longed for a fight.
   When fighting ensued
   This hapless dude
Went AWOL and left in a fright.

In the modern navy some brains are required.

The navy seemed just right for Jim,
He longed to get into the swim.
   Try as he might,
   Not being too bright,
Boot camp was too much for him.

Everyone can pick it up but not everyone can play it.

A fellow from St. Joe, MO
Played an old piccolo,
   His notes they would screech
   And all would beseech
The piccolo Joe must forgo.

Hey Jody, why don't you just move to England?

A Scottish guy Jody McTavish
Said, "I'm not living too lavish,
   The folks that live down
   In old London town
Are rich and we live rather hellish."

Old Mack knew a good way to finish it off.

The barbecue grill in the back
Was usually manned by old Mack.
   He'd fix up some meat,
    Add pickled pigs feet
And finally then a six-pack.

Did you notice that John Wayne just played John Wayne in all his movies? He always looked and sounded the same no matter who his character was supposed to be.

John Wayne said a man's gotta do
What he's gotta do to be true
   To his fan base
    And never disgrace
The image he painstakingly grew.

Redenbacher is now a well known name.

Orville R. was big in pop corn,
Pop corn by the truckload was born.
   He made it pay
    By the millions they say,
His name not now spoken with scorn.

Chapter 10 – PG Rated

There always seems to be a catch.

A man with a high haughty aire
Loved a babe who wore red underwear.
   They always made out,
   Then drank guiness and stout
Till his wife discovered the pair.

Do you know the legend of Dublin's Molly Malone who has been described as a fishmonger and sometime tart?

The fishmonger Molly Malone
Did some things most don't condone.
   Her cup size was D
   And as you can see
To buy her fish requires a loan.

<u>On this one the name has been changed to protect me.</u>

Billie Joe said it's not tough
To find one that has the right stuff.
   Never cull's what he said
   When he took them to bed,
You may find a diamond in the rough.

<u>Joe had the same problem as the guy on the previous page.</u>

Joe and his lover LaVern
Went at it at his place or her'n,
   There love it was strong
   Till she came along,
Joe's wife who did a slow burn.

These kinds of problems never seem to end, anyway what are friends for?

A young man named Charlie McRend
Busily wrapped packages to send,
   While His wife, a hot babe,
   Made love in the shade
To poor old Charlie's best friend.

I think about some of the strangest things when I watch Western movies.

Western movies never show
When folks on the trail have to go.
   Girls in long dresses
   Would make some big messes
And the sight would be disgusting I know.

When you pick up a girl you may be picking up something else.

Harvey Lewinsky Loo Met
Picked up a girl on a bet,
  She gave him much fun
  But when it was done
Gonorrhea was hard to forget.

I think this can be easily remedied.

We sometimes live to regret
Some of the girls that we've met,
  Like Missy La Due
  Who hadn't a clue
About where on a man she should pet.

Li'l Abner your not alone. (Once again I ask you to remember an old cartoon character, the hillbilly, Li'l Abner Yokum.)

Li'l Abner loves Daisy Mae
When she puts her chest on display.
  His heart fairly sings
    When those world class things
Are put on display every day.

Once again I have changed the name to protect me.

When Suckmore Swanson was a pup,
Never at the table would he sup.
  Though strange as can be,
    It's rumored that he
Was nursed till he could standing up.

Now you tell me!

A young man from Montana way
Set out to have a great day,
  He picked up a dame
  And danced until lame
But for more she said you must pay.

Lulu Belle and Scotty were performers on the National Barn Dance, a country show on WLS radio in Chicago during the 1930's and 40's. I don't think Lulu Belle would have actually done this.

Lulu Belle and Scotty were sure
There union would always endure.
  They never fought
  Until she was caught
Playing house with old Joe McClure.

I hope Jimmie was told in an age appropriate way.

Little Jimmie McLame
Knew not from whence he came.
  His Mama said
  It started in bed
And for you, your father's to blame.

If your name is Lurch, weird is a given.

Lurch was a weird son of a gun
Who was into weird things for fun,
  He dug holes with spades,
  Played pick-up grenades
And tried to play footsie with a Nun.

Or for that matter when its cold.

Elephants remember a lot,
Like where to poop and where not.
   It's good that they do
   'Cause no one wants poo
In places they eat when it's hot.

That's pretty dang cheap but then they were not very good looking.

Out on the western frontier
No lady would ever appear.
   The girls were all tarts
   And lacking in smarts
And most could be had for a beer.

I knew that Jack and Jill went up a hill but this puts a whole new perspective on it.

Jill would go up a hill,
Jack would go with a pill.
   They told no one
   What they had done
On the hill that made Jill so ill.

Miss Bream should be happy this was only a dream.

Mary Elizabeth Bream
Was having an intense dream,
   She was with a guy
   Who made her comply
With his every wish it would seem.

Once again, weird politicians.

The street by Joe's house was a mess,
City fathers said, "we confess,
  The money we saved
  From roads unpaved
Paid for ladies that we could caress."

I wonder where he hangs out.

I once heard a widower say,
"I miss seeing ladies each day.
  They look mighty fine
  With each curvy line
Thrilling me with their display."

This is as revolting a development as a husband can have.

The ladies of Lu's Sporting House
Were not known for wearing a blouse.
  Joe Brown thought this great
  But became quite irate
When one of the girls was his spouse.

Can we assume it was with Jane's consent?

Tarzan kept beating his chest,
"Me Tarzan", he said, "Me the best."
  His manners not good
  But I know that he would
Have his way with Jane in his nest.

Sue learned that it would pay cash.

The Lord in Heaven said hey,
To be a sinner won't pay.
  Sue missed the memo
  And put on a demo,
Got paid to let the boys play.

I guess there is not an age limit.

Old men will not go astray
If they are too old to play.
  Be that as it might
  By my good insight
If their able bodied they may.

Joe may be macho but he doesn't seem to have what it takes.

Joe, a macho man said,
"Can't get girls out of my head".
  Joe is obsessed
  With finding the best
But none will get into his bed.

Bird 1. loneliness and bird 2. poverty.

A lonely widow named Bone
Went to bed her skills to hone.
  With a rich guy,
  I think you know why,
It's killing two birds with one stone

<u>Throwing a bash is not a good reason for a loan.</u>

Emma Elizabeth Crone
Decided to take out a loan.
   She needed the cash
   To throw a big bash,
This reason they did not condone.

<u>There's more than one way to get a banker's attention. Some things trump a good reason. Loan granted.</u>

She came up with a new way to deal,
To the banker it would appeal.
   She'd meet him at night
   In very dim light
And all of her she would reveal.

Bruce decided it was worth a try.

Lina the Italian masseuse
Was massaging a man named Bruce.
  Bruce made a move
  Lina didn't approve.
She said, "Bruce you'd better vamoose."

That Robin Hood does more than just shoot arrows.

The Sheriff of Nottingham said,
"I'll see that Robin is dead".
  The Sheriff was steamed
  When it was deemed
That Robin took his wife to bed.

Good luck, Bill.

The ladies were loved by Bill,
His fantasies they could fulfill.
   The fantasies would
    Take wing if he could
Get them to bend to his will.

I find it hard to believe she just forgot.

"Oh my gosh" said Louise,
"My skirt flew up in the breeze,
   I forgot to wear
    Anything there
Underneath above the knees.

So recreation wasn't the only motivation for Jack.

Jack the dandy it's said
Took ten ladies to bed,
   Not just to sleep
   But also to keep
His reputation widespread.

It appears that apple pie was the only thing Ole liked about his wife.

Ole Wilson the sawmill guy
Just loved his wife's apple pie,
   Made every day
   Till Ole did stray
And run off with a lady nearby.

Isn't that typical of men marooned on an island?

Marooned on an island was Curt,
Shaken up but not really hurt.
   Ate tropical fruit
   And edible root
But longed for the sight of a skirt.

I think Lulu's trip was not meant only for a vacation.

A trip to an Alpine Chalet
Was routine for Lulu LaFay.
   She went for good cheer
   And sausage and beer
And made the boys happy each day.

Bill didn't deny it but definitely had a better story.

A right wing politico said
"Bill Clinton takes interns to bed."
  "I think so do thee"
  Said Billie with glee,
"But the intern you took was named Fred."

I suppose it's possible he couldn't tell them apart.

The lawyer said "guilty as sin,
The proof's in the brief I turned in,
  There is no doubt
  That this dreadful lout
Made love to his lovely wife's twin."

I suppose the Senator's wife did give up some prestige.

The right honorable Senator Mack
Couldn't resist taking a whack
   At giving some pearls
   To pretty young girls,
Not amused, his wife gave him the sack.

There are some things that trump bad music.

Ora Lee Jones played the drums
So bad that folks twiddled their thumbs.
   "But I'm a great fan",
   Said Ora Lee's man,
"I like what at night she becomes."

I suppose that's one way to look at it.

Darlene McCool liked to play
With her friend Jeff every day.
   Jeff's sinister plans
   To be done on divans
Was an anatomical buffet.

I'm with you, Joe.

Joe had hoped for a son,
His wife did not give him one.
   She produced a girl
   With a cute little curl
But to try again will be fun.